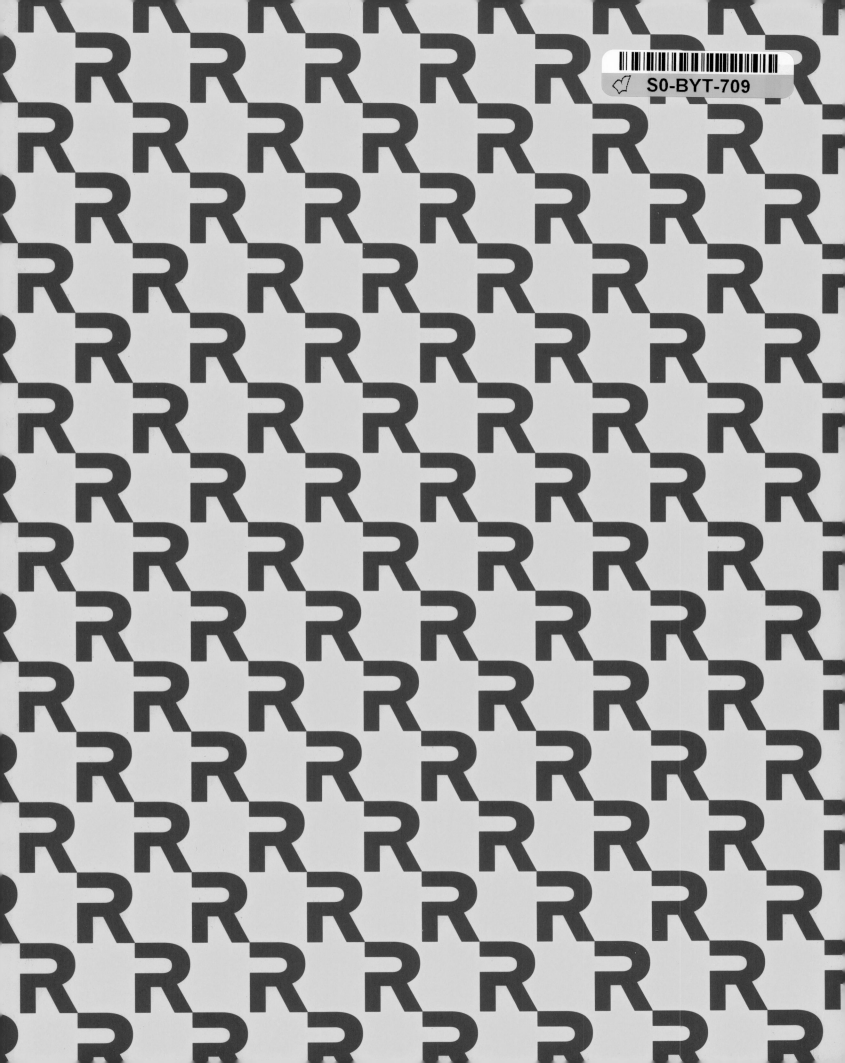

S0-BYT-709

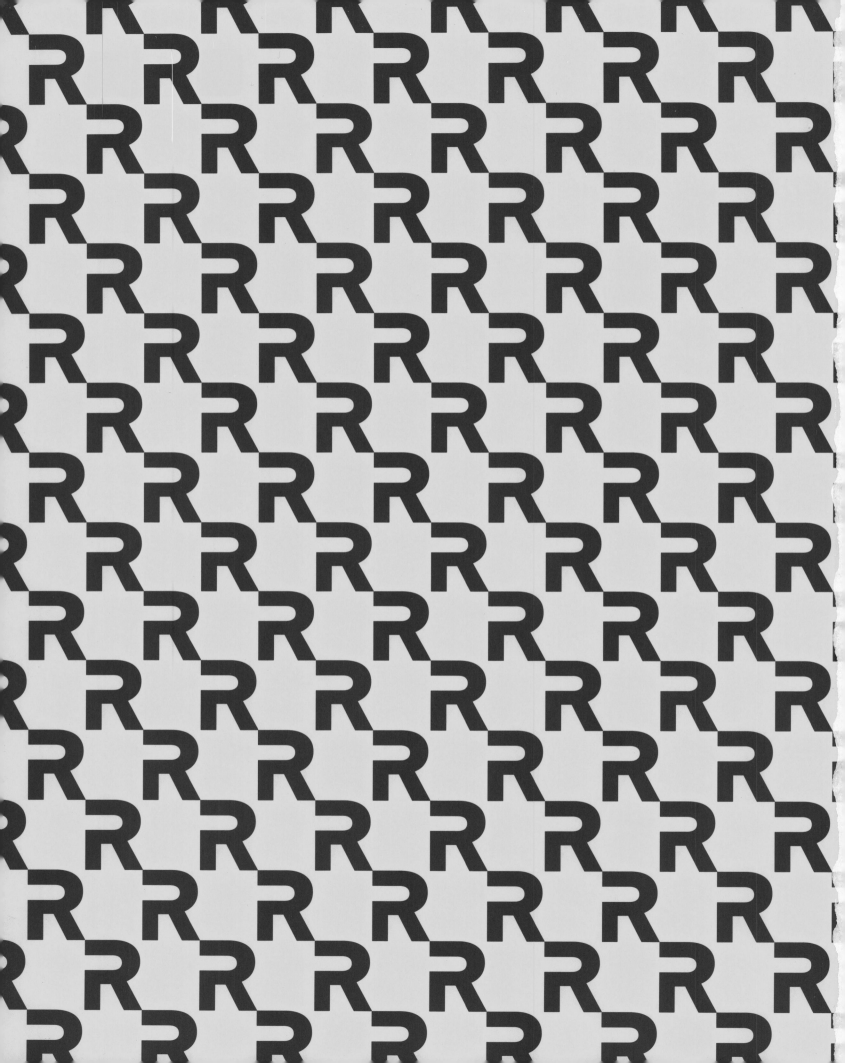

R
20

R & Company
20 Years of Discovery

Foreword

Foreword:
Pioneering Collectible Design

Evan Snyderman

It all started with a few simple questions: Who were the icons of the design world? Why were people collecting them? How could we find other, lesser-known designers? How could we establish or create our own icons? Designers such as George Nakashima, Charles and Ray Eames, Jean Prouvé, and Charlotte Perriand were already well-established in the market. But my partner Zesty and I thought there must be more like them out there.

The year was 1997 and interest in 20th-century design was growing. A handful of brave and passionate dealers had started collecting and selling mid-century design in the late 80s. However, values were low and documentation was sparse. We saw this as an opportunity, a field very early in development with endless possibilities. We quickly realized that since there was so much to be discovered, it seemed all we had to do was ask and doors would open up to us and information would pour out. This idea has guided us as a gallery since the very beginning of R & Company. The early discoveries we made on trips to California, Scandinavia, the Netherlands, and Brazil led us to understand the larger purpose design played beyond the practical and functional sense in societies around the world. We wanted to make design important, we wanted to tell the stories we heard on these trips. We had to preserve this history before it was too late.

There was little information to go on for us in those early years. There was no internet, just a handful of periodicals and a few overview books about 50s design, such as Cara Greenberg's *Mid-Century Modern: Furniture of the 1950s* and *The New Look: Design in the Fifties* by Lesley Jackson. We would pore over these books for hours. Then, the Christie's and Sotheby's auction catalogues started to come, and we learned what little we could through these limited research materials. On every trip we made, we would come back with three or four new books found at antiquarian book shops in foreign lands. Just prior to opening our first space in the Williamsburg neighborhood of Brooklyn, a picker friend invited us to apply for a space at the 26th Street flea market in Manhattan. We did so, and began in what was called the "Free Lot," at 25th Street. After a year or so, we graduated to the "Pay Lot." This was the big-time in the flea market game, where pickers and dealers fought every Saturday and Sunday before dawn to find a scrap of modernist treasure buried in a plastic bin or in the back of a dark van or U-Haul. We used to refer to it as the "Wild West," as it seemed there were no rules, just the law of the land. People would show up at the market with what was, unbeknownst to them, a rare piece of design; it would be instantly scooped up, then flipped sometimes once or twice before finally being sold to a dealer in Manhattan. In a way, I think back to those days as the "school of hard knocks." We learned the business through hard work, dedication, and curiosity, with a large dose of competitiveness. We also met some of the biggest cultural influencers at that flea market, many of whom are still friends and clients of ours today.

Toward the end of 1999, we started to have some success in our Brooklyn space; *Wallpaper* magazine had written about us, and people were coming to our space not just from Manhattan, but also from out of state and Europe. However, we knew that for us to grow and achieve the dreams we had of organizing exhibitions featuring some of what we had started to discover in our travels, we needed a bigger space. And we needed to move to Manhattan.

We left Brooklyn in 2000 just as Williamsburg was beginning to show signs of its current manifestation. We found a space on Franklin Street in TriBeCa where, at the time, several other design outposts, like Dune and Totem, were already established. When we moved in to the TriBeCa space, our program was strictly 20th-century design, however we had already developed a unique approach to how we displayed the work we exhibited. We preferred to organize things in a more livable environment, creating room settings or featuring works on pedestals instead of stacking things up or filling the floor with material the way many of the other 20th-century dealers were doing. Having been to art school, Zesty and I understood the importance of presentation and composition. We also knew how to talk about work more critically, how to explain the craft of an object, the technology used in its creation, and the idea behind the design. We had been traveling to Scandinavia and the Netherlands for several years already and had been building an inventory of pieces by a little-known Dutch designer, Cees Braakman. When we opened in May of 2000, with plywood still on the windows since construction was not yet complete, his was our first exhibition. Since that day, we have continued with the same spirit and drive to discover, pioneer new markets, preserve the stories and histories of the past through exhibitions and publications, and create genuine connections with our clients and the designers we represent.

So much has changed since that year, and R & Company has continued to grow and change as a business. With the introduction of our contemporary program we were able to develop a different level of connection with contemporary designers. We learned to invest in them and commit ourselves to finding new channels for their work to be seen globally through collaborations with museums, galleries, architects, and collectors.

The first contemporary designer we represented was our long-time friend and collaborator Jeff Zimmerman, a master glass artist. After his first commission of a chandelier for a prominent New York art dealer and collector, a lightbulb went on for us. Commissions offer new opportunities and challenges to our designers and can offer permanence to their work. With the introduction in 2005 of the fair now known as DesignMiami, everything started to change. It began with art dealers collecting work from our designers, but quickly spread to their art collectors as well. What changed was that for maybe the first time, collectors saw design not just as a functional object, but also as something that could become a part of their collection. Design had real value, and could also be enjoyed as a physical object, so they had, perhaps, a different relationship with it than with art that hangs on walls. Design is something meant to be touched, even sat on, and this is the inherent difference between the two worlds.

Over the past 10 years, as the gallery matured, we took on representation of some of the most talented contemporary designers working today. The list grows each year, but what remains the same is the shared vision and dedication to our diverse program. Experimentation and dialogue between the designers, the gallery, and the work itself constantly push us to do better and to break down categories or definitions of what design is or should be. We hope to carve out our own market rather than rely on an existing one. We strive to give the designers we represent our full attention, and present them on the global stage, giving them the support and space to try new ideas and forge their work forward. We have championed uniquely different designers, ones who choose not to follow the herd, not afraid to take chances and explore their ideas in whatever medium they choose in establishing their own voice in the world of collectible design. We have had the greatest pleasure working with Jeff Zimmerman, Wendell Castle, Rogan Gregory, Renate Müller, the Haas Brothers, David Wiseman, Thaddeus Wolfe, and Katie Stout, to name a few.

We've developed a niche in the design and art world, working closely between the two as the demography and tastes of our clients change. We are still only in the beginning stages of what we see as a new movement within the design world, one where ideas come first, not practicality or utility. A hybrid of craft, art, theory, and technology come together to make us appreciate the objects around us. From this vantage point, we now occupy a space we can call our own.

Throughout the past 20 years, our commitment to the designers, their ideas, and the level of presentation of their work has remained passionate

RETOLD: Bidjar Iron and *RETOLD: Tekke Madder* carpets, Dana Barnes, exhibited in *Woven Forms*, Palazzo Benzon, Venice, Italy, 2017.

SuperDesign, curated by Maria Cristina Didero and Evan Snyderman, 2017.

and focused. Zesty and I are constantly raising the bar for both our designers and ourselves. We are dedicated to preserving design history, from the mid-century through the present-day and into the future. Our passion drives us to constantly create new conversations that are meaningful and honest within the field of design.

As we move into our new gallery space on White Street, we now embark on yet another chapter. The scope of this building will give us the freedom to continue our exploration into historic and contemporary design and re-contextualize our constantly growing permanent collection. Within this new space we can elevate the work we exhibit once again to the next level, giving it the attention it truly deserves. This book offers the perfect bridge, with great writers from the field exploring some of the themes and movements that R & Company pioneered.

Part 1
Visual Identity

A Conversation with Design

Dan Rubinstein

When I walk into a design fair, no matter how many booths there are, or how many special installations there may be, it's a familiar experience. There's always new stuff to find—a color that's coming back, a historical style that's suddenly in vogue again, or pieces from a breakthrough star you haven't seen before—but the experience itself is usually the same.

However, when I step into R & Company's gallery, I really have no idea what I'm about to experience. I've been visiting that same space for more than a decade, and it's different every time. My expectations are always high, and they're always surpassed. The walls aren't 50 feet high. The front window is small and unassuming. Come to think of it, I can't recall what the floors are made of.

What makes R so exciting? It's a total package: built-out vignettes, elegant signage (or none at all), and works of design that feel like they were created just for that space, just for that exhibition. Even the catalogues are exquisite. In an industry that's undergone such dramatic growth and change, this gallery in particular has been at the center of it all, consistently deepening our understanding of and appreciation for design.

But it wasn't always this way. "Let's rewind 20 years," says Evan Snyderman, the gallery's co-founder and now its creative director. "When we started in this business, there was really no one producing exhibitions on design, or representing designers. It was just people selling vintage furniture, mid-century design. That's what brought us into this field—the idea of going out and buying things at estate sales or thrift stores and bringing them to market." Snyderman, along with [his business partner/co-founder] Zesty Meyers, started dealing in New York's flea markets before opening their first permanent space in 1997 in Brooklyn, a DIY-looking locale by today's standards. "There were other dealers," says Snyderman, "but we were the new kids on the block."

New kids, indeed. In R's full-page editorial in *Elle Décor* [that year], Snyderman, then just 27, was photographed pouting next to Meyers, then 28, who's hugging one of those globes you'd see in a high school classroom. The article even used a word you wouldn't dare associate with them today:

Façade of R & Company's 82 Franklin Street gallery with the original neon "R" that hung outside the first Brooklyn gallery and new hanging sign by Gabrielle Shelton, Shelton Studios, Inc.

retail. Especially because in the years before R, Snyderman and Meyers were originally artists themselves, members of a group called the B Team that melded live performance with glassblowing. The transition to becoming gallerists came naturally for both of them. "I don't think we had a choice, because of who we were, coming more from the art world. I'm a person who can't live with things out of order. I'm constantly adjusting chairs to line up. I can't stop. It's an obsession," Snyderman continues. "When we started in flea markets, we wanted to have the same kind of beautiful setting there that you'd imagine having in your home. We had such elaborate plans! But it worked. And it got people to come to our Brooklyn store."

Things grew from there. "We were one of the first galleries to approach the idea of presentation as an important aspect of the business, instead of just selling stuff on shelves," he says. The first exhibition in the gallery's TriBeCa space, which opened in 2000, was on Cees Braakman, a Dutch mid-century designer. "At that time, we were traveling to the Netherlands and shopping that part of Europe, and had discovered this person we had never known before. Everywhere we went, we would see more of his work," says Snyderman. "We saw an opportunity there. We wanted to discover things

AFTER, curated by Kelly Behun and Alex P. White of kelly behun | STUDIO, 2012.

that others had overlooked." That first show in the Manhattan space might be considered humdrum for the duo today. "It was simple. We hung some text and blew up some photographs. We recreated some of the imagery that had been used in catalogues in the 1950s to sell his work."

More prophetic of the future-to-be wasn't the decoration, but their detail-oriented obsession with documenting and producing content in an age before Google and social media. The young gallery rented a photo studio and commissioned elaborate recreations of Braakman's print advertisements to use in the catalogue. "We realized we had an opportunity to create or preserve a little bit of history," Snyderman recalls. Documenting work—with both an editor's and an artist's eye—has had a huge impact on the gallery's trajectory, both with clients, as well as in journalistic and institutional circles. Since then, the gallery has always had a photographer on staff. "We can really art direct every image that goes out, and oversee how things are perceived by the way we present them."

Fast-forward to today, and R & Company now plans their shows 18 months in advance. It sounds more like a museum than a showroom, with a staff of more than 20 that includes marketing and sales teams, a librarian and an archivist, and restoration and installation specialists. "Everyone's involved," says Snyderman. Today, he, Meyers, and their team can handle planning about half a dozen shows at a time. "It's a company-wide process that all starts with an idea."

One of the gallery's greatest ideas is to share its venue with other curatorial minds. Snyderman and Meyers's Guest Curator Exhibition series, which began in 2002 and now takes place every September, has outside designers, architects, and tastemakers create and curate their own shows. By bringing in outsiders to such a controlled environment, the very comfort zones of the business are expanded and cajoled. One that stands out in Snyderman's mind as a favorite was 2008's *Sticks, Stones, Bones* by New York–based editor and stylist Michael Reynolds. "That was one of the most incredible installations we've ever done," he says. "It was transformative because it was the first time we really brought in major things from other places. Michael wanted to show a 5,000-pound crystal and cover the gallery in wallpaper. He borrowed Roman busts and giant elephant tusks and skulls, and paired it all with our Wendell Castle and Italian Radical Design pieces and photographs by Victoria Sambunaris, a friend of his. The sad part was that the show opened the day Lehman Brothers collapsed, so we didn't sell a single thing. But it's never been about money for us. It's about creating a conversation."

When I recently entered the gallery for a tour of 2017's Guest Curator Exhibition, *Oops* by the Paris-based interior designer Pierre Yovanovitch, that conversation was evident all around me. Temporary walls were created, some painted in stark primary colors reminiscent of the late 20th-century Mexican architect Luis Barragán, whose earthy, minimal style is all the rage. Freshly built cornices spotlit ceramics by the Haas Brothers. This time, I noticed the floors instantly. They've been covered in a soft, faux black terrazzo that gave the space a sophisticated, postmodern edge. Newly created furniture pieces by Yovanovitch—sofas in complex shapes, fuzzy armchairs, blobby lamps that defy classification—mingled with painted, cactuslike totems by Lapo Binazzi. I was handed a bilingual catalogue printed on various paper stocks with moody, sumptuous photography of everything on offer. I was told that the build-out of the space took three weeks, with demands by Yovanovitch to fly in painters and craftsmen from France.

It's hard not to be impressed. Meyers said a quick hello as he dashed through the main space, but he couldn't help but show me the exacting beauty of his *Otto* desk and its sliding metal drawers that change the entire shape of the object when opened. "Pierre is the Jean Royère of today," he says reverentially. "Don't you think?" To his credit—and to Yovanovitch's—he's right on the money.

Inviting an interior designer like him to the gallery to present his own production furniture that he normally only produces for his own clients is a new development for the 20-year-old enterprise. But it's completely in line with where the contemporary world of design is at the moment. In doing so, R & Company is yet again helping to move the cultural conversation forward. "In my mind, our exhibitions are what have really set us apart," says Snyderman. "What drives us is the idea of presentation, of curating, and of putting things into context and creating immersive environments."

When I hear that the gallery is moving to a bigger space in the coming year, I ask him: Will you be able to keep up this level of quality with so much more space to fill? "We have endless lists of ideas for exhibitions," he says. "We're never going to get to all of them."

Floor lamps with "Cobra" shade, Greta Magnusson Grossman for Ralph O. Smith, USA, circa 1949.

Portfolio:
Visual Identity

above: *Quasidodo, La Brea Brad Pitt, Cheetah Hayworth, Fruit Stripe* and *Taz-Been* carpets designed
by The Haas Brothers (wall) and *The Journey* carpet with *Island* stool by Hun Chung Lee (floor),
exhibited in *Woven Forms*, Palazzo Benzon, Venice, Italy, 2017.
right: *Rain Flower* and *Rain Bird* carpets, Wendell Castle, exhibited in *Woven Forms*, Palazzo Benzon,
Venice, Italy, 2017.

Works by Wendell Castle, Oscar Niemeyer and Verner Panton, exhibited at DesignMiami, 2006.

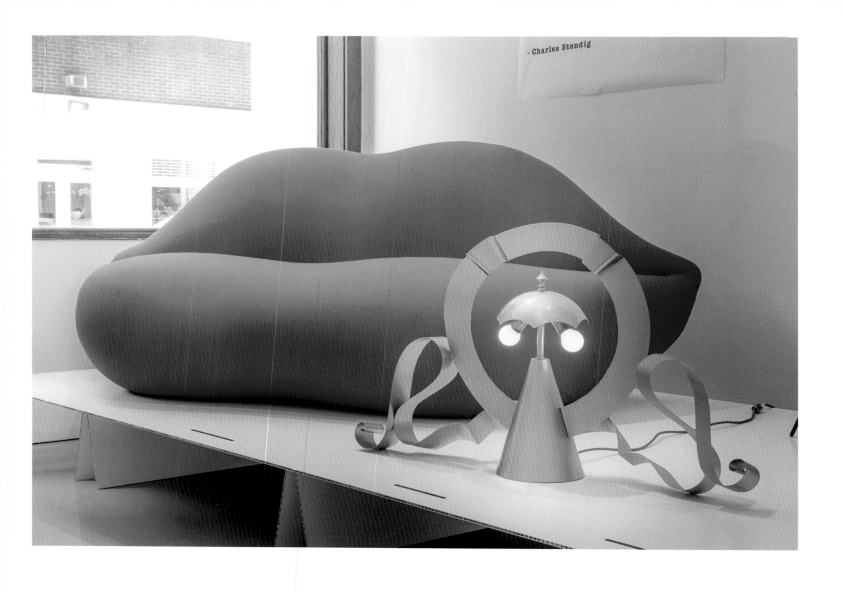

Difficult, curated by Jim Walrod, 2015.
Works shown by Studio 65, Lapo Binazzi, Gaetano Pesce and Gerrit Rietveld.

DIFFICULT

Curated by Jim Walrod

above: *Hung: A Century of Coat Racks*, curated by Zesty Meyers and Evan Snyderman, exhibition design by Claudia Dias, 2003.
left: *Greta Magnusson Grossman – A Car and Some Shorts*, curated by Evan Snyderman, 2013.

Thaddeus Wolfe: New Work, 2015.

Promotional photograph for R & Company's booth at DesignMiami, 2016 featuring works by Lapo Binazzi, Greg Chait, Martin Eisler, Katie Stout, Joaquim Tenreiro

WHA
17 SEPT

Well, what matters
encounter raw mate
transformation proc

Here, we celebrate
This is a fan letter, i
to the artists who e

We are fortunate th
an integral part of t
cooked up a few lir
— wood, glass, me

The best chefs alwa

On that note, Bon A

KULAPAT Y

why design

What's the Matter?, curated by Kulapat Yantrasast of wHY design, 2013.

S THE MATTER?
BER - 2 NOVEMBER

what we are excited about is how artists from many generations
h ancient and new, and through using their own unique tools and
w they investigate and explore these various 'ingredients'.

y and the brilliance found in the objects we all love and admire
of an exhibition, to the world of materials and processes, and
mploy them.

f our favorite artists let us borrow their tools and techniques as
, along with my team at **why design** and R 20th Century, also
n pieces. Our own investigation and experiments with materials
ne — produced fun results, all of which are on display here.

us, what matters most are ingredients, ingredients, and ingredients.

GAST

What's the Matter?, curated by Kulapat Yantrasast of wHY design, 2013.

OOPS, curated by Pierre Yovanovitch, 2017.
next: *Our Flag: Design Stands Together*, an exhibition to benefit the ACLU, curated by Zesty Meyers, Evan Snyderman and James Zemaitis, 2017.

OUR FLAG: DESIGN STANDS TOGETHER
#designstandstogether

Sticks, Stones, Bones, curated by Michael Reynolds, 2008.

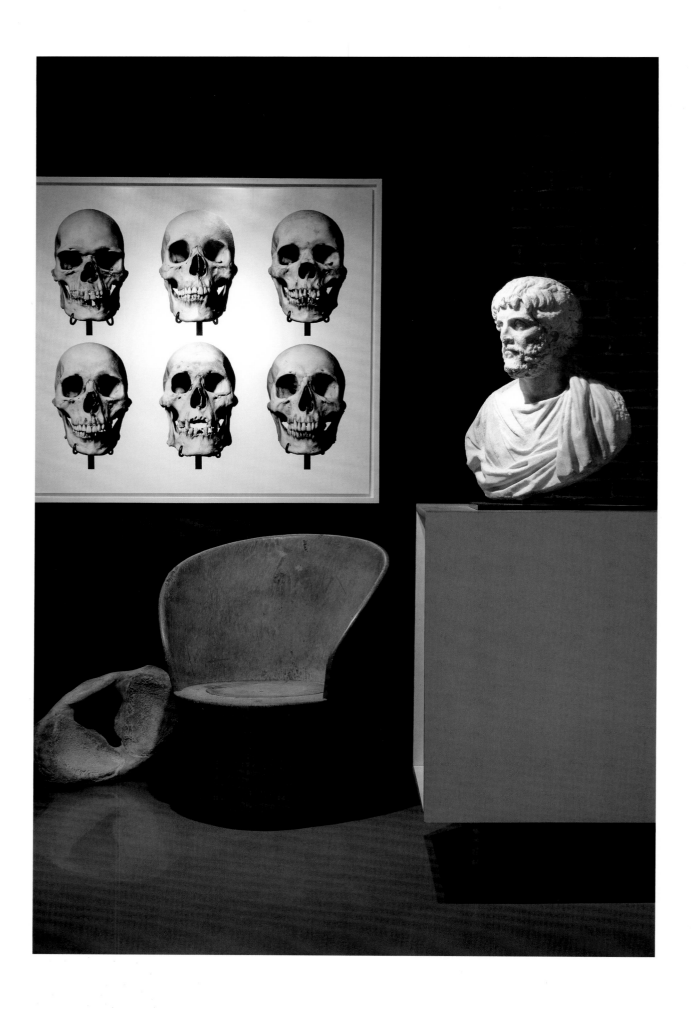

Sticks, Stones, Bones, curated by Michael Reynolds, 2008.

R & Company's 82 Franklin Street gallery, works shown by Poul Kjærholm, Kenji Fujita, Greta Magnusson Grossman, Pedro Petry, Wim Rietveld, Sergio Rodrigues, La Gardo Tackett, Joaquim Tenreiro, Jeff Zimmerman.

Part 2
Brazilian Design

Discovering Brazilian Design:
An Interview with Zesty Meyers

Dung Ngo

DUNG NGO (DN): Do you remember when you found your very first Brazilian Modern piece of design?

ZESTY MEYERS (ZM): Oh, I'll always remember. Before the Internet, we would buy antiquarian books for research. One day, Evan and I bought a book on Oscar Niemeyer, and we sat around and theorized that if he built the Modernist, utopian Brasília, there would have to be a local culture of designers that responded to the forms of the architecture. The country wouldn't have imported all the furniture for their capital city.

So, we simply started to ask questions and do our research. Antiquarian books from different countries of the time period would have a small, 2-inch-square picture that would say: "Joaquim Tenreiro, Brazil" or "Rio de Janeiro." Nothing more. This was the 1990s, like 1997 or 1998.

DN: So when you'd just started R 20th Century?

ZM: Yes. And from there we started asking people if they had any connection to Brazil: "Could you bring us a periodical? Anything?" Lo and behold a client of ours was married to a Brazilian, and lived half the year in the country. She shipped up a bunch of furniture to a studio in Long Island City and invited me to come see it all. I actually drove the van myself back then. I spent all the money I had that day. When I returned to Brooklyn, where the gallery was then, I took the *Mucki* bench by Sergio Rodrigues out of the van and just put it in the middle of our space. Evan and some clients were like: "What is it?!" Everyone was all excited, it was a new discovery. I started asking people what they thought it was, and people said: "Oh, it's French." "Oh, no, it's Danish." Nobody knew, which made me realize we'd found something that was unbelievable. All these people were smart, they were collectors, yet nobody knew who or what it was. I took the rest of the pieces in from the couple and told them: "You have to take me to Brazil."

DN: Give me a little context, what were you guys dealing in the late 1990s? What was your expertise at the time?

ZM: We were really known for Scandinavian design back then. By late

1996, we were shipping containers back to the U.S. before that market really existed. We could buy a whole 40-foot container with all the big names for under $10,000. We'd go to the Salvation Army in Sweden and Denmark and have to choose: "Should we take the Hans Wegner or the Arne Jacobsen? Because we're running out of room in the container."

Of course, we had American design, too. We had already decided that we would never really go after French design because all the French designers were already too famous and the dealers too established. And we

Tripé chair, Joaquim Tenreiro, Brazil, circa 1947.

would never really try to represent Charles and Ray Eames, because that work was already too known. But would I take in an Eames prototype? Yeah, of course, any masterwork from someone like that, or if we found the rarity or the oddity, I would be interested. But other people that were already popularized, not so much. We determined that if everybody knew who Alvar Aalto was, there had to be a second designer in Finland, which lead us to our early exhibition on Ilmari Tapiovaara.

Our research methods were really simple: We would find a book, and then get on a plane. Once there, we would do two things: First, we would look for dealers. Second, we'd find the antiquarian book shops. The first time we went to Finland, we asked the guy in a book shop about Finnish design and he said: "Oh, yeah, no one's asked me in 15 years." We bought a massive number of books from him. This is how we started to get our bearings. Even though we couldn't read Finnish, we could familiarize ourselves by looking at images, we could ask questions, and we were on our way.

That was our approach to Brazilian design, and it totally worked. Evan came with me for the first trip, around 2002. The first piece we bought was a Joaquim Tenreiro chair, one of his classics. It looks almost like a Windsor-type lady's chair, with a cane seat and little spindles, and it weighs almost nothing, like Gio Ponti's iconic *Superleggera* chair. At the time, I thought we were paying a lot for it. But when we brought it back and put it out in the gallery floor, it sold within a week to a collector in Singapore.

Seating, Lina Bo Bardi, Brazil, 1950s-1980s.

DN: Did you only buy from dealers on that first trip to Brazil? Or were you able to get into some private homes?

ZM: There weren't really dealers then as we know them now. No one showed furniture in street-level spaces because of crime. Everything was more hidden. But there was one flea market we visited that was filled with rosewood and caviona wood pieces, one more amazing than the next.

One night on that first trip we went to the home of the artist Tunga [Antonio José de Barros Carvalho e Mello Mourão] who died last year. He sat there and educated us until 4:00 in the morning about Brazilian design and why it is important. And what he knew, he really knew. He connected the works with history and culture.

I must have gone back to Brazil eight more times that year. And as I keep going back, I decided to put a 25-year discovery timeline on it, because I knew what we'd stumbled upon was massive. I knew we had a design culture that was very different than ours, so to get the information out was going to be very different than what I would do in Europe, and it would take me decades to uncover.

DN: When you encountered Scandinavian and then Brazilian design pieces, which differences between them struck you immediately?

ZM: That's a really good question. When you look at them separately, you think they could be the same. But they really can't. If you put a Brazilian chair next to a Danish chair, the Danish chair is so strict-looking and such a single school of thought, whereas the Brazilian chair is like a wild child.

DN: Why do you think that Brazilian designs are so much looser, freer, more...would you say sensuous?

ZM: It's definitely sensual. I cannot prove this, but my belief is because of where Rio lies on the earth, there's some magnetism or something that gives a feeling of freedom. There are American and European influences without a doubt. You find references in the work that indicate Brazilians understand the past and have studied the designs that came before them. But they are bringing it to a future in some kind of way, and using extraordinary native hardwoods in doing so.

DN: In your introduction to the book *Brazil Modern*, you wrote that one of the main drivers of Brazilian design is the immigration of Europeans right before the end of World War II. The first mature wave of Brazilian designers is actually European-trained.

ZM: Brazilian design took in every school you knew: German, French, Italian. And then mixed it with the culture of immigration. It's like the perfect storm. You have the intellectual student on the boat, the father probably had

hand skills, and the mother had the recipes. In Brazil, food grows like crazy, wood grows like crazy, and labor is cheap. It's the ideal working conditions. It's much easier to experiment when you have food, warmth, and material.

DN: It's an imported culture that's transformed by the local conditions: The climate, the landscape, the food transformed these European ideas into something else.

ZM: Also, these people were free in a different way. They weren't living in the cities that were so organized like the ones they grew up in. They were trying to figure out how to make something become "Brazilian." This became their new national identity. "We are now in Brazil. We have now found ourselves. This is what we're going to do going forward. We have this freedom to become ourselves." This started in the 1920s, but it really emerges in the 1940s, 1950s and 1960s, and it's still happening today.

DN: That's a good segue into Oscar Niemeyer. His idea of a native, Brazilian Modernism must have had this incredible influence on the other designers around, and Niemeyer commissioned Joaquim Tenreiro and Sergio

Brazil Modern, curated by Zesty Meyers and Evan Snyderman, 2015.

Rodrigues to furnish many of the buildings in Brasília. What was his influence on Tenreiro and Rodrigues, not just in terms of patronage but also in terms of form and the idea of Brazilian design?

ZM: The form didn't necessarily come from him. For many of the governmental palaces and civic buildings, designers were given a space and basically asked to come up with what they wanted. Some of it is absolutely mind-blowing. And tons of it is still there, still in use. Much of Niemeyer's furniture is still there, in particular, because it is placed in buildings he designed.

The organicism you feel when you think about Brasília instantly goes with the furniture. Tenreiro mimicked the forms and curves to a certain extent, but, in balance with his own style, which was rigorous in its precision and craftsmanship. Rodrigues's designs were more, in a sense, for the people. He was the heart of Brazil. He used the thicker, chunkier wood, beautifully cut and shaped into rectilinear forms with some organic curves. He used the best of these materials and forms, making it just slightly more executive and statesmanlike, while maintaining a sense of approachability and comfort.

It must have been a dream to have that level of work to use in the civic buildings, and so much of it. When people think of Brasília they think: "Oh, wow, it's utopia when you go there." It's a giant small city, these buildings are enormous. And they didn't commission one piece from these designers, for many it was the biggest commission of their career.

DN: Let's talk more about Tenreiro. He was born in Portugal and then moved to Brazil when he was young, so there's some European roots to him. How would you compare his work to the Europeans of his generation?

ZM: Let's break it down a little bit. In my estimation, he was one of the five best designers in the world from the mid 20th century. His limitless ability to keep creating masterworks is something I've never seen. Who else would I put in this category? George Nakashima would be one. Carlo Mollino would have to be another, the craziest. But Tenreiro, he produced on the prolific level of Gio Ponti. I recently saw pictures of custom Tenreiro pieces at an estate—so many of them I'd never seen before. There's no record of them, no sketches anywhere.

One of the other great things he did was he was always nodding toward the past. His three-legged *Tripé* chair was his masterwork. The scale of it is like an Art Deco slipper chair, but, by making it more triangular, it almost looks like it's taking off for space. It gives the illusion that it's moving fast because it's striped and carved and the legs carry your eye upward. But the height and the scale is everything that's French Art Deco, like something that would be in someone's bedroom or bathroom from that time.

He was obviously looking around—the Wiener Werkstätte must have been an inspiration. His works have the caning, or proportions, that you would see from the Wiener Werkstätte, and he focuses on the understructure. Using his immense skill as a woodcarver, he added details that you would never consider being there, nearly out of view. Why is he doing that? Because he's playing with your eye. He's getting you to focus on something: Why is this chair more attractive than what I've seen in my whole life? Why is it just that much better?

Instead of having just a standard colored-glass top on a dining table, let's say, he would instead reverse-paint the glass top, so that the color would really suck you in. If the whole thing was solid, it would push you away. He's playing with the glass by a millimeter or two sometimes, to get you to look more closely and bring you into his world. Or, if you've touched a leg of his chair, it would be beveled in four different directions. But you can't see it with your eye. You have to touch it to get it. It's absolutely amazing.

DN: Obviously the woods that Tenreiro used are native to Brazil and that makes it very Brazilian. What about the construction of these furniture pieces: How do they compare to the Danes, which are the closest comparisons we

Chairs and dining table, Joaquim Tenreiro, Brazil, circa 1960.

can make in the post-WWII era?

ZM: The Tenreiro furniture has the craziest joints you'll ever see in your life. If you show it to a woodworker, he'd say it was impossible, the time it would take to carve some of the joints. Plus, there's no structural need to execute it at that level. It would take 100 or more hours to make a chair or table the way he did. But he kept pushing and pushing himself; he was almost obsessed with the craftsmanship. The Brazilians didn't have the sophisticated woodworking machines that the Europeans had. Somehow, they figured out the strength of the material or the skill of the carver just by trying and doing. They would get to know the material and how it moves intimately. By the way, the same thing can be said about much of Sergio Rodrigues's work as well. The joinery is really, really good.

DN: I wonder if these complicated joints have to do with the fact that they were producing furniture in and for a tropical climate? It's humid and hot, the material would expand and contract, so you have to have stronger joints in order for it to actually withstand the climate stress.

ZM: The glue that was used during this time—the 1940s through the 1960s—was made to lock tight with moisture because of the humidity you mention. When the pieces come to the U.S., we have to deconstruct the whole piece and re-glue every single joint because the glue just dries up.

DN: So this is how you know how complicated the joints are?

ZM: Yes. And this is how we can also tell if something is copied. Because you can see in copy of a Tenreiro piece that the joints are not as well made.

DN: Let's move on to Sergio Rodrigues. He's 15 years younger but in some ways a whole different generation from Tenreiro: Much freer, much more open. What was his education, did he study as a designer?

ZM: He did. Tenreiro grew up in a more conservative culture than Rodrigues. Rodrigues's family was political—activists and intellectuals. He was born in Brazil, grew up with that background, and just started to make his own work that people bought into. I think by this time, he's referencing the land, Rio particularly, which is at the center between the north and the south, so it is the heart of culture in Brazil. Sergio often would tell me how in Rio everything comes up from the sea.

For instance, if you take a look at his *Diz* chair from 2001, it has a sort of mobility about it, like it's walking. Once, he took me through the history of the chair. It actually began around 1960, with a chair he designed for his grandmother called the *Stella*. When you look at the *Stella* chair in profile, you can see the basic lines of the *Diz*. He then showed me the seven or eight iterations it took to finally got to the *Diz*, but it took him 40 years. That reveals how he had the freedom and the passion to keep experimenting.

DN: Another difference between Tenreiro and Rodrigues is that Rodrigues mass-produced certain designs for a larger market rather than solely custom or commissioned designs.

ZM: The furniture chain he started, Oca, was the DWR or the IKEA of its day. These stores were giant. The factory was giant. It employed most of the young people getting out of architecture or design school at the time because there was no other work. But it didn't work as a business in the end. Sergio was more of a designer, a true artist, than a businessman.

DN: For me, what's so interesting is that, again, the difference between Brazilian design and Danish design is, like you said, the Danes were importing rosewood and all the precious wood from South America and Brazil. But in Brazil, that's the one resource they had in spades.

ZM: Yes, it's amazing. Brazil has around 3,000 species of native woods. For centuries, people were using rosewood—how many palaces around the world have furniture and detailing in that wood? Rosewood is now making a comeback because it is being successfully farmed. It will be much better in another 10 years because the trees grow so slowly. But rosewood will be back for people to buy, which is fantastic.

DN: Speaking of wood, I want to talk about José Zanine Caldas. If there's a desire on these designers to find the spirit of Brazilian design through its wood, would you say that in some ways Zanine is the one who captured it the best?

ZM: Zanine started off as a model-maker for Lúcio Costa and Oscar Niemeyer. He never got a degree in architecture, but built hundreds of houses—massive, crazy, huge houses in some cases. The stories of him go that he would build someone a house, go away, and then come back in a pickup truck saying: "Here's your dining table," or "Here's your bench." Obviously, people commissioned him, too.

He didn't use any one species of wood. He would go and find wood. He'd say: "Oh, I'm driving down this road and they're cutting down these trees." And he would find a way to pick up the wood and start making things from it.

You can sort of track Zanine through this body of work. He kept moving to different parts of Brazil, and the styles would change as he moved. His early company, the Z Móveis Company in the 1950s, was furniture for the people. Then later, from the 1960s to the 1990s, he starts making the giant pieces he's known for.

DN: For me, Hugo França is a spiritual disciple of Zanine, very much working in that tradition.

ZM: Yes, his work is probably even freer. Hugo really works with the tree. There's definitely some reference in scale or massiveness, but Hugo's done something I think is very different and unique. Hugo's work gets to a point where it's not even him—he's communicating through the tree.

DN: What do you think is the future of collectible Brazilian design?

ZM: It's blowing up. I think we're only at the humble beginning of what will happen globally in terms of collectability. You have auction houses chasing it down. You have dealers all over the world trying to get a hold of anything and selling it. You have the fakes coming along, which I despise. But people are hungry for work beyond what we've started. I can't grow a market if other people aren't interested. Museums are taking more interest, they're coming after pieces. We're starting to place them for perpetuity.

I feel we are only halfway through the period of figuring out "What is Brazilian design?" Maybe my 25-year discovery period wasn't even enough time. In some ways it has become a part of my life's work. I think there's so much more to come.

Portfolio: Brazilian Design

Promotional photograph for *Lina Bo Bardi + Roberto Burle Marx*, curated by Zesty Meyers and Evan Snyderman, 2015.

Joaquim Tenreiro, curated by Gordon VeneKlasen, exhibition design by Annabelle Selldorf, 2013.

above: Table and chair, Joaquim Tenreiro, Brazil, circa 1958.
right: Seating, Martin Eisler and Carlo Hauner for Forma, Brazil, 1950s and 1960s.

Mesa Parker custom dining table and chairs, Sergio Rodrigues, Brazil, 1978.
previous: *Marquesa* bench (2007/08), *Rio* chaise (2001) and coffee table for Tendo Brasileira (2008),
Oscar Niemeyer, Brazil.

above: *Milhazes* game table (1988), *Cuiabá* chairs, mirror and console (1985), Sergio Rodrigues, Brazil.
Boccia hanging lamp, Luigi Caccia Dominioni for Azucena, Italy, 1969.
left: *Tonico* armchair (1963) and *Mucki* benches (1958), Sergio Rodrigues, Brazil.

Bonded wood stools (circa 1950), custom rocking chair (1948) and custom wall-mounted console (circa 1955), Joaquim Tenreiro, Brazil.

Joaquim Tenreiro works exhibited at DesignMiami/Basel, 2011.

Dining table and stools, José Zanine, Brazil, circa 1970.
right: Promotional photograph for *José Zanine*, curated by Zesty Meyers and Evan Snyderman, 2016.

Side and coffee tables, José Zanine, Brazil, 1950s.

Part 3
American Historical Design

Discovery and Rediscovery:
The Evolution of the American Design Market

James Zemaitis

I remember my first visit to 82 Franklin Street as if it were yesterday. It was the autumn of 2000. I was between auction house gigs, living in the West Village, scrounging for freelance work from the new wave of internet design magazines. I'd heard about an exhibition at a gallery called R 20th Century on the Swedish-American designer Greta Magnusson-Grossman, and I walked downtown to investigate.

There were several takeaways from this exhibition. First of all, how on earth had I not heard of Greta Grossman until now? I had never seen her work in an auction catalogue, certainly not in New York. She wasn't included in my weathered bible, Cara Greenberg's *Mid-Century Modern: Furniture of the 1950s* (1984). Nor was there an entry on her work in the seminal museum exhibition catalogue, *Design 1935-1965: What Modern Was* (1991), edited by Martin Eidelberg (which, in retrospect, is quite extraordinary, considering its emphasis on the confluence of mid-century American and Nordic design). She was not present in a concurrent exhibition at the Bard Graduate Center, *Women Designers in the USA 1900-2000*, although her career was discussed in a single paragraph in the accompanying catalogue as "Greta Von Nessen's counterpart on the West Coast" (apparently because they were both Swedish-born and named Greta).

Secondly, I walked away from this exhibition, at a mid-century modern gallery, with an academic catalogue in my possession, containing professional photography of the objects in the show, period Julius Shulman images of her California residences, and a full-fledged bibliography. Not only that, but the gallery had made its publishing debut (and TriBeCa launch) earlier in the year with a catalogue on the obscure Dutch plywood designer Cees Braakman, and it was planning a third on the Finnish legend Ilmari Tapiovaara. Icing on the cake: Evan Snyderman and Zesty Meyers had already conceived of the catalogues as a boxed set triptych, with a unified graphic identity! It was like George Harrison's *All Things Must Pass* for the design market.

Finally, I was knocked off my feet by the organic shapes and color

"Grasshopper" floor lamps, Greta Magnusson Grossman for Ralph O. Smith, USA, circa 1948.

palette of Grossman's lighting designs, which I discovered were produced in California (and Sweden too, but not yet emphasized in the gallery) by a small machine shop in Burbank. As an East Coast resident, I was inclined to think of Charles and Ray Eames as being more Michigan than Los Angeles, and the first wave of American mid-century designers who were starring at auction—the Eames, George Nelson, and Isamu Noguchi—reflected a New York perspective and bias. Suddenly, a window was opened for me on what I might have missed out West.

In order to understand R & Company and the scholarship and market for American design today, it is important to trace the origins of the community of American galleries, auction houses, and publications that existed 20 years ago. First of all, the New York dealer Mark McDonald and his partners at Fifty/50 played an outsize role in presenting American postwar design to an elite circle of serious collectors and museum curators as part of their more expansive focus on international Modernism. Their debut show at

their second space at 793 Broadway, *Charles and Ray Eames: The Sum of the Parts* (1983), was the first-ever Eames exhibition to include Charles's wife Ray in the title. Although there were other notable New York dealers who specialized in vintage design, including Robert Swope and Michel Hurst (of Full House) and Bill Straus (of Upstairs Downtown), McDonald's connoisseurship and curated exhibitions at both Fifty/50 and Gansevoort Gallery, his 1990s Meatpacking District landmark, gave him preeminent status as the official mentor for the next generation of dealers, many of whom started in the Chelsea Flea Market: Andy Lin and Larry Weinberg (whose 1997 exhibition on Edward Wormley produced the first academic catalogue on American mid-century design by a commercial gallery); Patrick Parrish; Gerard O'Brien; Adam Edelsberg; Jim Walrod; and Snyderman and Meyers. Inside the aluminum gates designed by Ali Tayar, these guys and

left: Chair designed by Charles Eames and Eero Saarinen for *Organic Design in Home Furnishings*, curated by Elliot Noyes at the Museum of Modern Art, New York, 1940. Manufactured by Haskelite Corporation/Heywood-Wakefield, USA.
above: *Ball* clock (Howard Miller, circa 1949) and desk (Herman Miller, 1948), George Nelson Associates, USA.

a small group of auction specialists including myself, the Englishmen Simon Andrews (of Christie's), and Alexander Payne (of Bonhams/Phillips) received our education in the Pioneers of Modernism.

Of course, the market was developing across the country, too. In Chicago, Richard Wright was organizing auctions at Treadway Gallery. Every Midwestern city had its dealer, with the store designs usually emphasizing the vernacular kitsch of mid-century "Googie" architecture and the nostalgic collections of "boomerang modern" compiled in Greenberg's guide, which, in retrospect, illustrates the influence of 1980s postmodern style, especially color and pattern, on the collectors and dealers of mid-century modernism. There were dozens of annual shows held in community centers and school auditoriums, where design was retailed as "collectibles," whether it was Eames plywood or Eva Zeisel dinnerware. The opening nights were occasions for the local Hepcats and Bettys to dress up in turquoise sport jackets and

coral skirts with black polka dots as if they were extras in a Stray Cats video. Mid-century modern was an actual retro lifestyle, and today the only show to retain traces of this 1980s-1990s community is Palm Springs Modernism.

California played a major role in the formation of the modern design market, with a natural emphasis on regional historic works, and a collecting lifestyle which was based on the restoration of mid-century residential architecture. Peter and Shannon Loughrey's Los Angeles Modern was the first American auction house to hold specialty auctions in this category. There were several dozen active dealers in the state, several of whom specialized in the work of Eames. And the power couple of modernism was Michael and Gabrielle Boyd, whose collection was exhibited at SFMOMA in *Sitting on the Edge: Modernist Design from the Collection of Michael and Gabrielle Boyd* (1998). The accompanying exhibition catalogue, together with *100 Masterpieces from the Vitra Design Museum Collection* (1996), codified the chair as the preeminent form of modernism, and served up American masterworks by Eames, Saarinen, Noguchi, and Nelson on the same level of importance as their European counterparts. The Boyds' collection, which was equally strong in Marcel Breuer, Gerrit Rietveld, and Jean Prouvé as it was the Americans, reflected a collecting sensibility that emphasized MoMA's mid-century canonization of the Pioneers of Modernism. This focus was shared by the programming in McDonald's galleries, as well as in the collection of the legendary New York dealer Barry Friedman, who maintained a weekend Breuer house in Croton-on-Hudson chock full of Eames, Nelson, Charlotte Perriand, and perhaps most influentially, several zoomorphic chairs designed by Carlo Mollino and the Californian Dan Johnson. Friedman's interior was photographed in Greenberg's book, which was the first exposure many of us had to these eccentric visionaries.

The culmination of the late 20th-century market for American mid-century design was a series of prominent auctions organized by Christie's in New York (where I was a cataloguer) and London, first on the modern chair, and then on masterworks of modern design. The works were sold in chronological order, from Josef Hoffmann to Marc Newson. At the midpoint of the sales were the finest and rarest examples of American design to ever appear at auction, and the prices, for an incredibly rare Noguchi *IN-70* sofa or a unique Eames plywood sculpture, soared into the six figures. In response to these high-profile sales, regional houses specializing in mid-century modern produced at least three Eames-only auctions between 1999 and 2001. Records were broken and prototypes were acquired by museums, but it was inevitable that a market dedicated to only a handful of the most famous designers, most of whose pieces were mass-produced for decades, would cool down as quickly as it had heated up. Meanwhile, at the local level, two guys in Brooklyn were buying and selling these American icons in their gallery, but on their van trips across the country, they were starting to

left: Stack-laminated cherry chair (1965), *Baker* arm chair (1967), *Wishbone* chair (1968), Wendell Castle, USA.

discover the "blue highways" of historical American design, the roads less traveled by their contemporaries.

The new millennium was a watershed moment for the modern design market. A few months before I walked into the R 20th Century gallery to view the Grossman exhibition, Richard and Julie Wright launched their eponymous auction house in Chicago, which represented a stunning improvement in the visual presentation of furniture and objects via the most important selling tool of the era, the printed auction catalogue. A few months after my gallery visit, Alexander Payne organized the first curated modern design auction at Phillips, and I quickly joined him at the firm to produce *Pioneers of American Modernism* in New York in June 2001. It was the result of several trips made to California, visiting the collections of the Boyds and Mark Haddawy, where I decided to organize an auction containing not only Eames and Nelson, but also the California-based architects Richard Neutra and Rudolph Schindler. The glue that bound everything together was a series of California-produced white-glazed modernist ceramics I kept seeing in period Shulman photographs of houses in the desert. Upon returning to New York, I distinctly recall an enthusiastic discussion with Snyderman and Meyers about the joys of Architectural Pottery. I managed to acquire a group of them on consignment, and arranged a photo shoot on the roof of the Phillips building. R 20th then pitched in and contributed the now-iconic desk designed by Grossman in 1952 for the manufacturer Glenn of California. The auction was a success, and my friendship with Evan and Zesty was cemented.

In 2002, R 20th with architect Steven Learner presented the exhibition *Outside*, which envisioned a mid-century Hamptons beach house outfitted with Architectural Pottery and lounge furniture by Van Keppel and Green. More than just an imaginary fusion of Atlantic and Pacific mid-century coastal residences, it continued the gallery's focus, like the earlier Grossman exhibition, on exploring the lesser-known but museum-worthy designs found in period publications including *Arts & Architecture* and the "Good Design" checklists of MoMA.

The final chapter in the gallery's evolution from its traditional mid-century modern roots to a more holistic approach to curating American design would arrive in 2004, with Donald Albrecht's exhibition *Autoplastic: Wendell Castle 1968-1973*. Snyderman, who grew up working at his parents' gallery in Philadelphia, had been exposed at an early age to the sculptural stacked-laminate wood furniture of Castle as well as many other key figures of the American Studio movement. In the late 1990s, with Castle marooned in postmodernism, and the sputtering market for the first wave of American furniture, glass, and ceramic makers trapped in their own auctions, fairs, and museums, Greenberg published her long-awaited sequel, *Op to Pop: Furniture of the 1960s* (1999). It was a groovy slap to the face of the modern market, with colorful spreads dedicated to Verner Panton, Gaetano Pesce, and the previously unheralded pop plastic furniture of Castle. At the same time, the auctions at Phillips, Wright, and Rago-Sollo in Lambertville, New Jersey, began to include the furniture of George Nakashima, Wharton Esherick, and the early woodworks of Castle as part of a seamless narrative of design which did not distinguish between modernism and craft. Prices for these historical makers exploded. But plastic was still unappreciated, and R 20th followed its wildest gallery installation to date, on Panton, with a serious academic study of Castle's inspired departure from the woodshed.

R's first exhibitions and catalogues on Grossman and Castle were the defining moments in the gallery's history of American design scholarship. With Grossman, it led to the acquisition of her estate and archives, and the subsequent major retrospective and catalogue of her work which travelled to multiple museums between 2010 and 2012. The gallery's early focus on Castle's plastic designs resulted in an enduring partnership with the designer and led to the acquisition of numerous Castle masterworks in wood, and the collaboration with the Aldrich Contemporary Art Museum on the most important exhibition in Castle's 60-year career, *Wendell Castle: Wandering Forms - Works from 1959-1979* in 2012.

Two decades later, we have come full circle on the most iconic American mid-century designers. Auction houses must follow new trends, yet museums are still acquiring works by Eames, Saarinen, Nelson, and Noguchi for their permanent collections. Thanks to the gallery's efforts, Grossman has certainly joined the ranks of this top tier of designers who are essential for any serious American public collection, and it has become the gallery's mission to acquire major pieces by all these designers with the express purpose of placing them in institutions. Meanwhile, the search continues, whether that means visiting an estate, combing the gallery's extensive archives and library, or seizing the moment when today's generation of flea market dealers post their finds on Instagram, for the next important discovery of historical American design and craft which is worthy of exhibition, publication, and passion.

Portfolio:
American Historical Design

Greta Magnusson Grossman – A Car and Some Shorts, curated by Evan Snyderman, 2013.
previous: *Outside*, curated by Zesty Meyers and Evan Snyderman, exhibition design by Steven Learner, landscape design by Lindsey Taylor, 2002.

Outside, curated by Zesty Meyers and Evan Snyderman, exhibition design by Steven Learner, landscape design by Lindsey Taylor, 2002.
previous: *Greta Magnusson Grossman – A Car and Some Shorts* at Arkitekturmuseet, Stockholm, Sweden, curated by Karin Åberg Waern and Evan Snyderman, 2010.

Greta Magnusson Grossman – A Car and Some Shorts at Arkitekturmuseet, Stockholm, Sweden, curated by Karin Åberg Waern and Evan Snyderman, 2010.
next: Table lamps, Greta Magnusson Grossman for Ralph O. Smith, USA, 1948-49.

Untitled floor lamp in gel-coated fiberglass-reinforced plastic with flocking, *Fat Albert* floor lamp, *Molar Group* floor lamp and *Benny* floor lamp, 1969, exhibited in *Wendell Castle: Wandering Forms — Works from 1959-1979*, at the Aldrich Contemporary Art Museum, Ridgefield, CT, curated by Alyson Baker and Evan Snyderman, 2012.

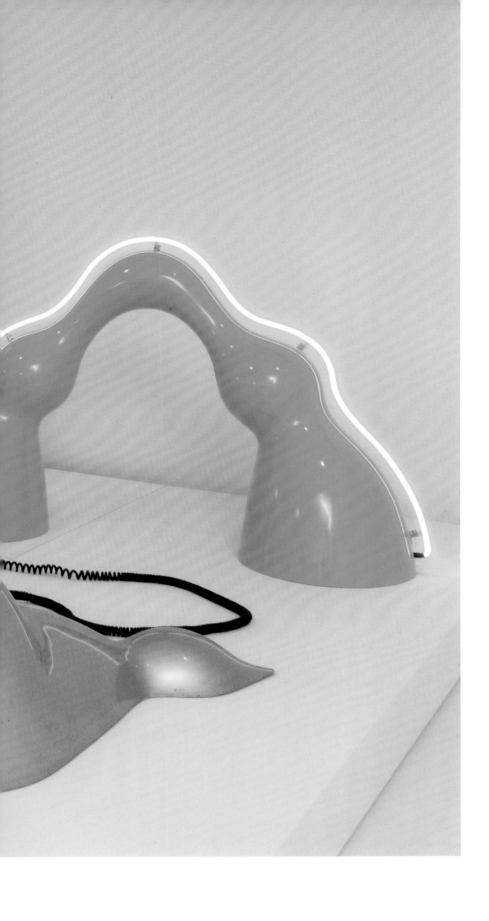

Chest of Drawers (1966) and *Enclosed Reclining Environment for One* (1969), exhibited in *Wendell Castle: Wandering Forms — Works from 1959-1979*, at the Aldrich Contemporary Art Museum, Ridgefield, CT, curated by Alyson Baker and Evan Snyderman, 2012.

Architectural Pottery by John Follis, Rex Goode, Malcolm Leland and La Gardo Tackett, USA, 1950s.
previous: *Big Red M*, originally designed by Wendell Castle for Marine Midland Bank, Rochester, NY, 1971. Shown exhibited in Grant Park, Chicago, IL during Public Art 2016.

Molar Group Baby Molar chairs, Wendell Castle, USA, 1969.
previous: Promotional photograph for *Blenko: From the Collection of AA Bronson*, 2001.

right: *XXe siècle: Salon international de mobilier & objets* (International Fair for Furniture & Objects),
Le Carrousel du Louvre, Paris, 2003. Works shown by Evelyn Ackerman, Milo Baughman, Luther Conover,
Greta Magnusson Grossman, Richard Neutra, Gio Ponti, La Gardo Tackett, photographs by Julius Shulman.
previous: *Table/Bench/Lamp* (1969), *Leotard table* (1968), *Neon lamp* (1969) and *Sluggo lamp* (1969),
Wendell Castle, USA.

Stack-laminated walnut table, Wendell Castle, USA, 1971.

above and right: *Charles Hollis Jones: Seeing Clearly*, curated by Zesty Meyers and Evan Snyderman, exhibition design by Calvin Tsao of Tsao & McKown, 2002.

Part 4
"Difficult" Design

The Discomfort Zone

Pilar Viladas

In my career as a magazine editor and writer, I have covered a significant amount of design that could be considered provocative, political, or just plain strange—that is, "difficult" design. Among the highlights: Ron Arad's automobile-seat *Rover* chair; Shiro Kuramata's metal-mesh *How High the Moon* chair; Robert Venturi's laminate-covered plywood homages to 18th-century English chairs; the renegade designs of Ettore Sottsass and his fellow members of Memphis; Roy McMakin's disquieting riffs on American domesticity; Gaetano Pesce's anthropomorphic resin pieces; and the Campana brothers' wood-scrap *Favela* chair. On the Dutch design scene, there was Hella Jongerius's passion for imperfection, as in her rubber *Soft Urn* vase for Droog, and the deconstructed decoration on her Nymphenburg porcelain; Maarten Baas's burned furnishings; and Studio Formafantasma's investigations of natural materials like Sicilian lava or plant-based polymers, and social issues like sustainability or colonialism. London, too, was alive with experimentation: Martino Gamper's remixed Gio Ponti furniture; Max Lamb's obsession with materials, from the logs cut from his grandfather's old ash tree to Styrofoam scraps; Faye Toogood's animistic approach to everything from chairs to shirts; or Study O Portable's cerebral designs and the thematic exhibitions—like *Pieces* (2015) or *Image for a Title* (2012)—that it organizes under the name Workshop for Potential Design. Back home, there was David Wiseman's eerily beautiful dining room ceiling, on which porcelain pomegranates hang from sinuous plaster tree branches, and Aranda\Lasch's focus on digital technology and new materials, which often produces remarkably sensual results. And that's just the tip of the iceberg.

Much as I love the classics of 20th-century Modernism and the elegant, inventive work of today's best industrial designers—I'm writing this at one of Eero Saarinen's *Tulip* tables, while seated on Edward Barber and Jay Osgerby's polypropylene *Tip Ton* chair—I'm also partial to the different, the challenging, and the downright weird. As I looked back on my enthusiastic support of the not-always-easy-to-like, it occurred to me that I've never really had to defend it. It was, after all, my job to show the new, even if it wasn't always nice, or polite. Not that this was a burden; I felt lucky to be able to show that someone was thinking about design in a new way, even if that work

right: *Dollaro con Wolkswagen*, Lapo Binazzi for Casa ANAS, Italy, circa 1975.

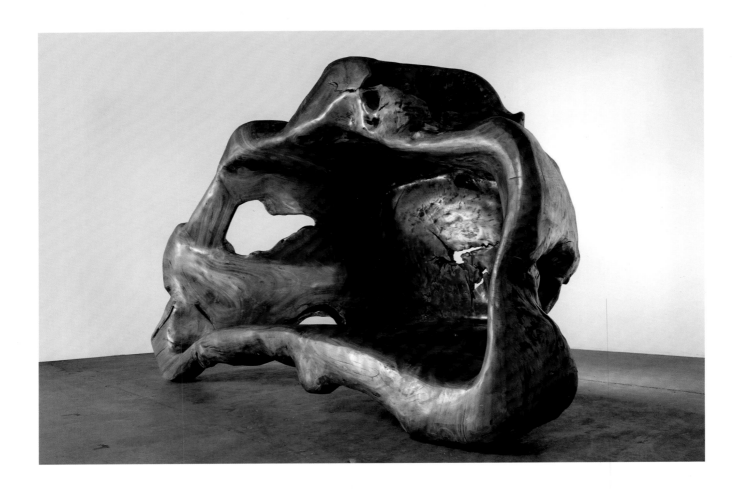

made me (or my readers) uncomfortable at first. I was, and am, grateful when someone upsets the apple cart.

So, in the early 2000s, I was encouraged to see R & Company (then known as R 20th Century) embrace the notion of "difficult" design. In parallel with their ongoing exhibitions of Modernist legends like Greta Magnusson Grossman, Poul Kjærholm, and then-lesser-known Brazilian masters like Sergio Rodriques and Joaquim Tenreiro, the gallery showed Jeff Zimmerman's startlingly biomorphic blown-glass lights and Hugo França's monumental chairs and sofas sculpted from giant tree roots, along with Wiseman's ever-expanding universe of natural forms rendered as lights, vessels, and furniture in bronze and porcelain. Soon, the roster of contemporary designers grew to include the Haas Brothers—whose work encompasses everything from furniture in the shape of furry, often frankly sexualized creatures to ceramics that combine delectably-colored (and high-tech) glazes with complex, multilayered textures—as well as Rogan Gregory and his abstract sculptural representations of the natural world; Thaddeus Wolfe, with his hard-edged, richly colored glass pieces; and Katie Stout, whose playful takes on ordinary domestic objects include a rug in the shape of a hat. Indeed, the gallery's

above: *Casulo Cariru*, Hugo França, Brazil, 2011.
right: *Rover*, Ron Arad for One Off, England, circa 1981.

2015 exhibition *Difficult*, curated by Jim Walrod, examined the process by which design initially outrages arbiters of taste but eventually becomes accepted and ultimately valuable, thereby putting an official name to this current.

At the same time, the gallery highlighted the innovative work of those who pioneered "difficult" design, who grew up in Modernism's heyday but rebelled against it. Wendell Castle, better known for his virtuoso work in wood, created provocative plastic furniture, like his famous *Molar* chair, in the 1960s and 1970s; Verner Panton's brightly colored plastic chairs and chandeliers made of what looked like giant gumballs thumbed their noses at International Style minimalism. More recently, a 2016 exhibition on Lapo Binazzi offered a survey of the Italian designer's subversive work from the 1960s to the present, in which popular imagery was used to critique a commercialized culture, as in his famous table lamp in the shape of a dollar sign. The show also offered a lead-in to *SuperDesign*, the gallery's 2017 exhibition examining the Italian Radical Design movement of the 1960s and 1970s, of which Binazzi was a key member.

What practitioners of "difficult" design, both young and old, have in common is their commitment to upend the status quo and push the boundaries of accepted good taste. 20th-century political and social upheaval, and a simultaneous rejection of Modernist orthodoxy, produced designs like Studio 65's *Capitello* chair of 1971, a foam seat shaped like a

lopsided Ionic capital, and Sottsass's *Ultrafragola* mirror, a 1970 design of acrylic and pink neon that was an abstract reference to the female anatomy.

Contemporary designers, faced with the return of political unrest and, if anything, an even more insidious strain of consumerism, are just as forceful in their responses. What looks like a lovely crystal cluster in the British artist and designer Paul Elliman's 2012 work, *Baby You Could Have Whatever You Like* (from Workshop for Potential Design's 2012 exhibition, *Image for a Title*) is actually fragments of clear-plastic Bic pen carcasses—a haunting commentary on the mountains of waste generated by our throwaway society. And Sottsass's mirror looks tame by comparison with Stout's *Girl Lamp*, which literally upends the decorative cliché of the feminine figurine as table lamp. Stout's version gives us a nude female figure standing on her head, her legs spread wide to support the lampshade; the electrical cord descends from below the shade, enters between the figure's legs, and emerges from her mouth. Take that, radical Italians.

As Walrod stated in his exhibition, "Today's difficult design eventually becomes tomorrow's collector's item." But even as our perceptions and social norms change, even if the work in question no longer seems quite so shocking, it still possesses the power to make us question our assumptions about function, beauty, the very nature of design, and its role in our lives.

Tawaraya boxing ring sculptural seating unit, Masanori Umeda for Memphis, Italy, circa 1981.

Portfolio:
"Difficult" Design

MGM lamp, Alchimia, 1980s; *Paramount* lamp, UFO, circa 1969; *Dollaro* lamp, Alchimia, 1980s, Lapo Binazzi, Italy. next: *Sassi* rock seats, Piero Gilardi, Gufram, Italy, this example circa 1986; *Cactus* coat rack, Guido Drocco and Franco Mello, Gufram, Italy, this example circa 1986, *Fireball* Lamp Type E, Verner Panton, J. Luber AG, Switzerland, 1970.

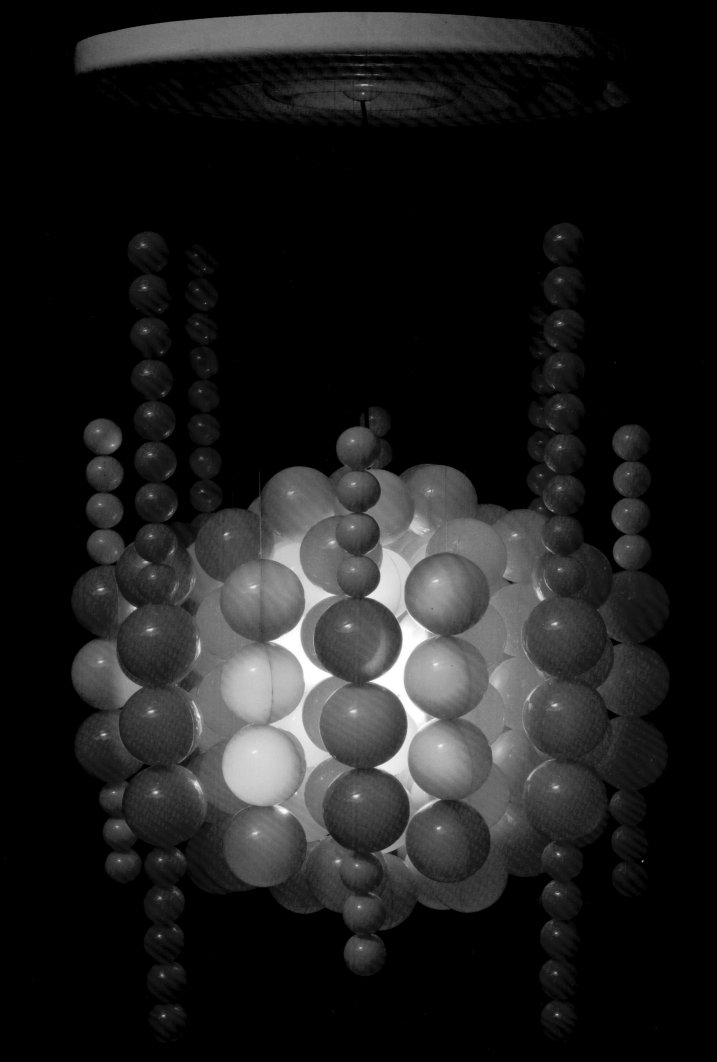

right and next: *Verner Panton*, curated by Zesty Meyers and Evan Snyderman, wall coverings from Maharam, 2001.

Molar Group Cloud Shelf, Wendell Castle, USA, 1969; *Pratone* lounge chair, Pietro Derossi, Giorgio Ceretti and Riccardo Rosso, Gufram, this example from 1986. Shown exhibited in *Blue Heaven*, curated by Tony Ingrao, 2016.

above: *Fiore Artificiale*, Gino Marotta, Italy, 1967. From the collection of Charles Stendig, NY.
left: Works by Wendell Castle, Oscar Niemeyer, Verner Panton and Joaquim Tenreiro, exhibited at DesignMiami, 2006.

Big Beaver armchair, Frank Gehry, 1987.

Promotional photograph for *Lapo Binazzi*, curated by Evan Snyderman, 2016. Works shown: *Doric Temple*, UFO, 1971, remade 1980s; *Dollaro* lamp, Alchimia, 1980s; *Paramount* lamp, UFO, circa 1969; *Neon Flower*, 1985; *MGM* lamp, Alchimia, 1980s.
next: *Porky Hefer: Heart of Lightness*, 2017, exhibited in collaboration with Southern Guild gallery, South Africa.

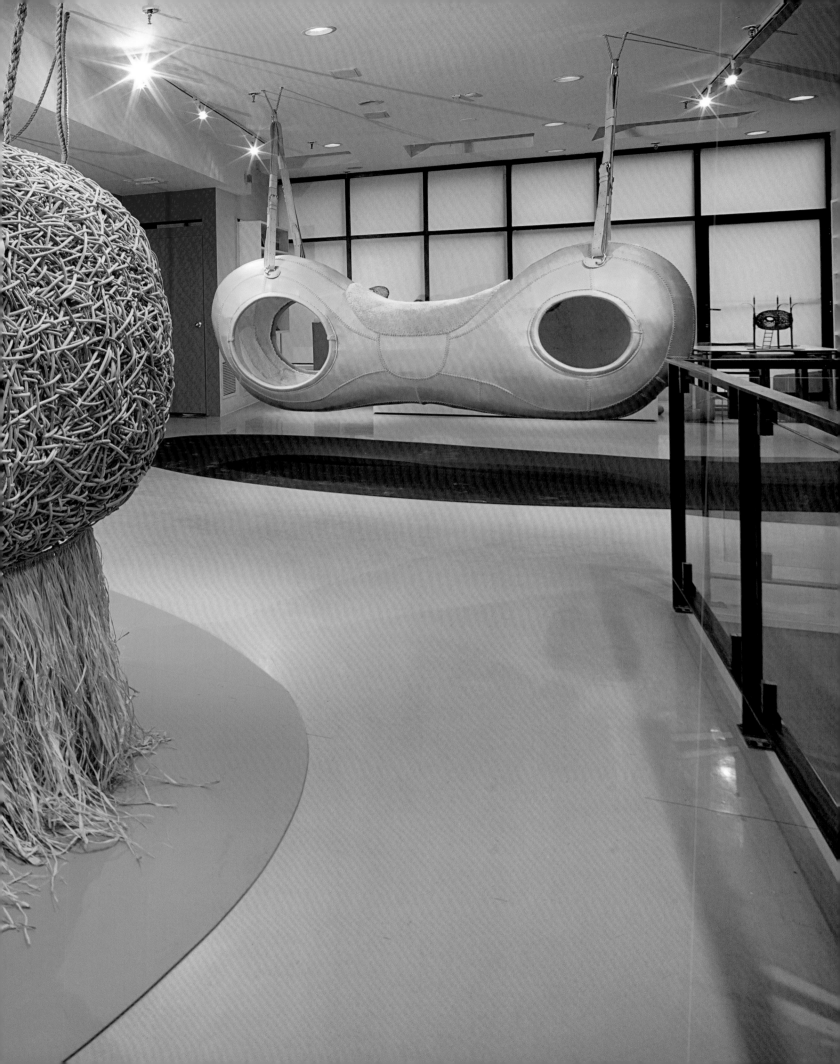

Lighting designed by Superstudio: *O-Look*, Poltronova, Italy, 1968; *Passiflora*, Poltronova, Italy, 1966; *Lampada Alabastro*, Italy, 1972; *Polaris Excelsior* lamp, Poltronova, Italy, 1967.
previous: Works by Porky Hefer exhibited in *Grains of Paradise: Contemporary African Design*, in collaboration with Southern Guild gallery, 2015.

Safari sofa and *San Remo* floor lamps, Archizoom Associati, Poltronova, Italy, 1967-68.
next: *SuperDesign*, curated by Maria Cristina Didero and Evan Snyderman, 2017.

Part 5
The Contemporary Atelier

The Materialists

Glenn Adamson

Much has been written, in recent years, about the implications of digital technology for design. The range of effects is quite extraordinary to consider. Most obviously, there are new tools for fabricating—3-D printing and the like—that open up possibilities in countless directions. Linked to these new processes is the question of scale. Unlike traditional factories, digital manufacturing platforms can be effective within very small runs, and constant variation can be introduced across a series, resulting in "mass customization." The impact of communication technology is also disruptive, in that it allows designers to collaborate with clients and partners worldwide, instantaneously, swiftly eroding local frames of reference. And, there is also a purely aesthetic dimension to the digital shift. Certain forms previously unthought—think asymmetric blobs and slippery morphologies that were not dreamt of even by the futurists of the 20th century—are becoming dominant in our visual environment.

A further repercussion of digitization, one that is less obvious but perhaps even more far-reaching in its importance, is the decline and fall of categorical thinking. Perhaps you remember the first time you entered a search term into a library's computer database. In that instant, what might have taken years of study to notice—the mutual relevance of studies from wholly different disciplines—was suddenly conjured, as connections between books stored under different subject headings were made immediately evident. The whole world is now like that. Instead of laboriously constructed frameworks, each clearly labeled and divided from its neighbors, we now inhabit an infinitely flexible information network.

Museums are still organized according to medium, but presumably that won't last long. I once worked at the V&A in London; the textiles were mostly in deep storage, pots were out on open display, and paintings somewhere on rolling racks. Needless to say, amazon.com doesn't organize itself that way, nor does the V&A's searchable object database. Viewed through the online portal, the institution's wealth of artifacts, all 2.2 million of them, effectively inhabit one plane, devoid of hierarchy or prejudice. Already, the galleries at the V&A and other museums are beginning to follow suit, with arrangement by associative themes rather than rigid classifications. That tendency will only pick up speed in the years to come.

right: *Line Relief Pendant*, Thaddeus Wolfe, USA, 2015.

The upshot is that many previously intractable debates, including those concerning design's relations to art and craft, are already largely irrelevant. We once needed to know where things were kept, and what they were called, so that we could find them. This no longer matters. Where something is kept and what it is called do not matter either; indeed, continuing to cling to those distinctions—or to terms like industrial design, studio craft, or design art—is simply an unhelpful limitation. All such categories do is to obstruct the process of adventitious discovery that drives the present.

The dissolution of categories occurred first, and is still most evident, in the arena of circulation. When you encounter something on social media, you tend to engage it on its own terms, not as an example within a larger set. You may care about who made it, how, and where, but only as part of its specific narrative; you don't need a label to pin it down, you can always find it again. But this flexibility has no exact parallel in the physical making of things. Just as museums, which are very path-dependent institutions, are struggling to reimagine themselves to suit the new dispensation, processes of manufacturing have a great many factors built into them, too. That means it is hard for makers themselves to simply embrace the whirlwind.

It takes a long time, and much expense, to learn skills, acquire tools,

Crumpled sculptural glass vessels, Jeff Zimmerman, USA, 2014.

and build out a suitable workspace. All those forms of investment militate against flexibility. Someone who has spent years training in woodwork and has a whole shop fitted out to do it is unlikely to drop everything and go weave baskets. The same friction attends art schools, which increasingly find it difficult to commit to specialist equipment and skills-building; that is partly because dividing an institution up into medium-specific categories just seems backward-looking, but mainly because of the resources required.

What all this amounts to is a somewhat counterintuitive phenomenon. The makers who are distinguishing themselves most within our rapidly changing digital environment are those who work in an assertively materialist fashion. It's comparatively easy to capture the tenor of the times in a website, much more difficult in wood, concrete, or metal. Those who do manage to navigate the hyper-fluid present through physical means achieve a resonance that was perhaps impossible even a decade ago; for never before has our bodily, experiential domain seemed more in need of imaginative inhabitation.

It is against this admittedly broad backdrop that a gallery like R & Company should be understood. While its represented designers are an eclectic group, all are finding unique ways to revalue material form. Often, they do so by hybridizing longstanding métiers and new technology. Wendell Castle is the representative figure of this transition. His career has been extraordinary in its length and richness, but perhaps the most lasting of his contributions has been the freeform sculpting of furniture, beginning in the late 1950s and maturing in the late 1960s—a breakthrough made possible through the process of stack lamination. The shapes he discovered back then have now re-emerged in the 21st century, bigger and, in some respects, better than ever.

Nothing will ever outdo the classic early Castle forms, with their subtle choreography of serpentine arcs and modulated masses. But the octogenarian maker is still pushing the limits, using a router on a CNC-guided robot arm to realize objects of increasing scale and complexity. Because he can manipulate and subdivide his designs digitally, prior to carving them, he is now able to make intricate puzzle-like constructions, move shapes around through cut-and-paste, and even duplicate and flip a form so that it mirrors itself perfectly. Try that with a hand chisel. Yet looking at these astounding new objects, one also senses the benefit of long experience; they are accumulations of Castle's own know-how. The lamination lines perceptible in his works could not be more appropriate, for each is a stratigraphy of methods: a few borrowed from historical woodworking, many invented by Castle over the decades, and more discovered through his recent interaction with digital fabrication. Technology has caught up to him rather than the other way around.

Many of the contemporary designers whose work R & Company has exhibited share Castle's infectious enthusiasm for experimentation. Among them is David Wiseman, who has long been entranced by the possibilities of patterning—he affectionately recalls poring over his grandmother's folio reproduction of Owen Jones's *Grammar of Ornament*. Just as Castle reinvented furniture via the carved mass, Wiseman has done so through the logic of "intelligent decoration." By this term, I mean an approach to embellishment that extends itself across surfaces and articulates them, unpredictably but satisfyingly. He works in a bewildering variety of media, and though there are referential aspects to his vocabulary (and an obvious love of decorative art history), he avoids straight revivalism. Thus, when creating a ceiling, he might nod briskly in the direction of 18th-century plasterwork, but the overall composition will have a life of its own, which brings his work right up to date. Though the means Wiseman is using are entirely analog, the effect has the searching, exploratory quality of the digital landscape.

A common thread among the R & Company program is just this uncanny and often humorous subversion of any inherent design logic. If Wiseman's

Bower Bird serving tray, David Wiseman, USA, 2016.

animated décor has the elegance of vintage Disney, then the works of the Haas Brothers veer closer to the madcap genius of Dr. Seuss. Twins who collaborate across a range of materials, Nikolai and Simon are possessed of demonic productive energy. The quintessential Haas Brothers object is a mash-up, combining materials associated with luxury—gilding, cast bronze, marble, blown glass—with elements that would be at home in a child's bedroom—thick fur, colorful banded knit. The resulting objects populate space more forcefully than most living people do; they are psychological presences with which one must contend.

There is an interesting and instructive comparison to be made between their work and that of Katie Stout, another R artist who is at an early stage of her career and perhaps reflects a new generational perspective. The juxtapositions in the Haas Brothers' work are vividly improbable, the comedy broad. They have the force of new discovery, and speak to the taste of a generation unleashed from both modernist strictures and the tormented ironies of postmodernism. Stout's work is equally free of these frameworks, but it is more, as they say these days, chill. Her forms have a gentleness, a slacker aesthetic, relaxed and pleasurable. These are objects geared to the quick, intuitive response rhythms of social media. Yet it was not just her undeniable charm that won Stout the widely-televised Ellen's Design Challenge on HGTV. She is a consummate craft-maker, both skilled and inventive, as is attested by her witty play of materials like paper pulp, and her refreshingly direct work in clay (often in collaboration with Sean Gerstley). Stout is definitely one to watch.

Thus far, I have been discussing designers who range widely across media; even Castle, who is so strongly associated with wood, has been deeply involved with plastics and cast bronze. That kind of material mobility is encouraged heartily by R & Company as one way that designers can signal their freedom from restrictive categories. But open-ended thinking is by no means incompatible with concentration on a single discipline, as is evident in the work of the gallery's artists Thaddeus Wolfe, Jeff Zimmerman, and Rogan Gregory. These three makers focus on just one or two processes: mold-blown glass in Wolfe's case, blown glass in Zimmerman's, and for Gregory, direct carving in wood or stone, and casting in bronze. Each is directly involved in the making process; they do not simply hand their designs off to fabricators. In that respect, all conform closely to the studio craft model that emerged in the mid-century era.

Yet in the domain of form, these three makers achieve an undoubted contemporaneity. One could indeed be forgiven for thinking that all of them create their work using digital fabrication techniques. Wolfe's totemic glass objects land on a plinth like alien objects fallen from orbit. Visually, they draw equally from raw geology and the intricate, pixel-by-pixel logic of the virtual. Some viewers may not even grasp that they are looking at glass at all—the substance of the work seems wholly novel. In fact, they are blown into irregular molds which themselves are cast from handmade Styrofoam sculptures. This multi-step process imbues the objects with a certain degree of misdirection, translating them into a mysterious, sensual artificiality.

Jeff Zimmerman's work in the same medium has a nearly opposite quality: The glass is obviously handblown, but pushed to the very boundary of technical possibility. An extraordinarily skilled artist, Zimmerman creates diaphanously thin volumes which fold and slump, as if caught in a moment of incipient collapse. Like Wolfe's much more gradual process of casting, this daring application of traditional skill produces a result that is profoundly futuristic, an effect that he exaggerates through the addition of colored and metallic surfaces.

Rogan Gregory is again opposite to this, adopting an approach to carving so primordial that his objects strike one as ancient precursors to more familiar, more narrowly functional things. Of the designers under discussion here, his work seems least in conversation with digital space, except perhaps in an oppositional sense, a reminder of the importance of physicality, weight, and tactility. Yet the perfectly smooth lines of his artifacts do, in fact, resemble the curvature of certain digitally designed buildings. In the architectural context, such seamless integrity has come to seem a bit of a cliché, but Gregory's insistence on the specific qualities of his materials—not just wood, but this particular wood—fends off any hint of banality, making each object seem essential, inevitable, born not made.

Each in their own way—Wolfe, Zimmerman, and Gregory—offer us opportunities to connect to something which we should never have lost track of in the first place: The pleasures of raw stuff in the hands of someone who knows what to do with it. While we all seem to be on our phones all the time at the moment, nearly all of us began life in a state of highly attuned material connection, and we surely need to return to it eventually. That is the nature of our first explorations of the world. It is why we give our children soft toys, before they are even old enough to talk.

It is interesting, in this connection, that R & Company represents the work of Renate Müller. She is a prominent toy designer, close to Castle's age, with a long and distinguished career in Germany. Aesthetically, it was not necessarily a great leap to introduce Müller to the gallery—one can easily imagine her creatures cavorting under a Haas Brothers mushroom. But even so, it took imagination to see how her work would fit conceptually into the mix. Pablo Picasso famously said, "It took me four years to paint like Raphael,

right: *Hex* stools and *Steven Tiler* bench, *Lana Del Frey Mini Beast*, *Goldie Fawn Mini Beast*, The Haas Brothers, USA, 2016.

but a lifetime to paint like a child." Perhaps our relationship to objects is somewhat like that, these days. As we are lured further and further into the digital realm, and the horizon of the material world recedes from our attention, we do need to be reminded of some simple truths. If it takes a cute stuffed rhino to do that, so be it. Great design can blaze new pathways we never expected to find. It can also give us what we have always wanted, and will never tire of. At its best, great design does both at once.

Portfolio:
The Contemporary Atelier

Custom *Elephant* benches. The Haas Brothers, USA, 2013, shown in a private residence, Miami, FL.

JEFF ZIMMERMAN

this page: *Jeff Zimmerman*, 2014.
previous, left: *Trans-Sep09L01* floor lamp, Jong-sun Bahk, 2009; *Concrete Day Bed with Ceramic Pillow and Jar*, Hun-Chung Lee, 2010; *Unique bench*, Hun-Chung Lee, 2009. Shown exhibited in *Contemporary Korean Design*, curated in collaboration with Gallery Seomi, 2010.
previous, right: *Jeff Zimmerman: New Work*, 2007.

Fertility Form table lamps, Rogan Gregory, USA, 2016.

above: *Girl Mirror*, Katie Stout, USA, 2016.
left: Custom flatware and cabinet, The Haas Brothers, USA, 2014. Shown in a private residence, Miami, FL.

Accretion vessels, promotional photograph for *The Haas Brothers: King Dong Come*, 2016.
previous: *Accretion* vessels and *Young Willing & Table*, The Haas Brothers, USA, 2016.

above and right: *Fertility Form* pendants, Rogan Gregory, USA, 2016.

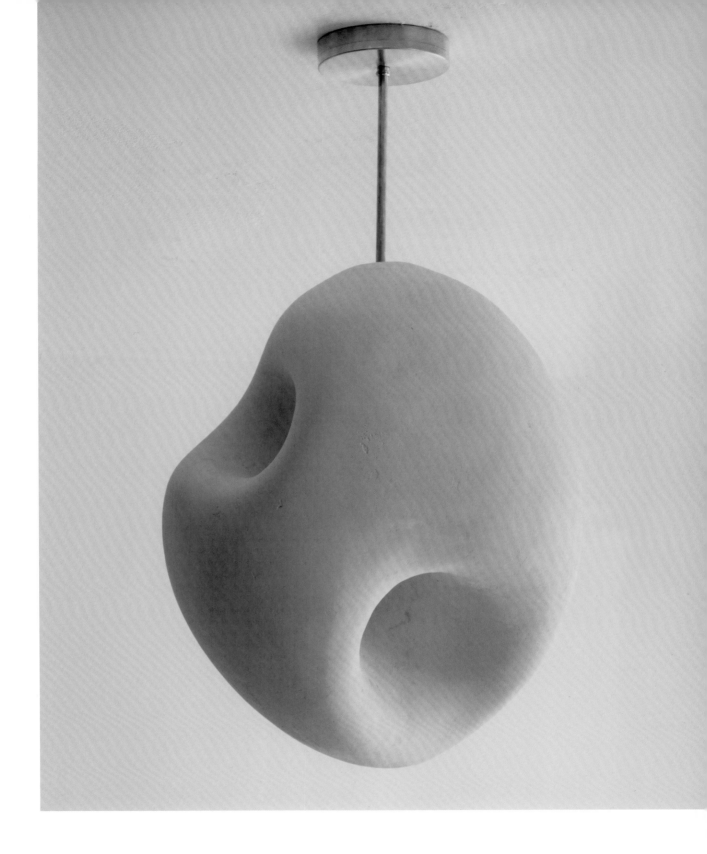

Beast club chair and ottoman, The Haas Brothers, USA, 2013.
previous: *The Haas Brothers: Cool World*, 2014.

Sculptural coffee table/*Polar bear* form and sculptural *Gorilla* form, Rogan Gregory, USA, 2016.
previous: *Animal Party* phosphorescent print in collaboration with Flavor Paper, shown exhibited in *The Haas Brothers: Cool World*, 2014.

above: *Illuminated Crystal Cluster*, Jeff Zimmerman, USA, 2016.
left: *Jeff Zimmerman: New Work*, 2011.
previous: *Red Tipper Gore, Rip Horn, Al Gor-illa, Bill-iam Oneyearbor, Mary Tyler Spore, Tail-or Spliff, Fungus Humungus, Fungul-iver, Neil Tongue, Tail-or Swift, Al Spore, Bench Fry, Eyes-Ik Newton, John Lith-cow* and *Fartin Odeur*, from the *Afreaks* series, The Haas Brothers and The Haas Sisters, South Africa, 2015.

Girl Lamps, Katie Stout, USA, 2017.
next: *Thaddeus Wolfe: New Work*, 2015.

Custom *Vine* illuminated sculpture, Jeff Zimmerman, USA, 2007.
previous: Wall-hung *Splash* sculptures, Jeff Zimmerman, USA, 2017.

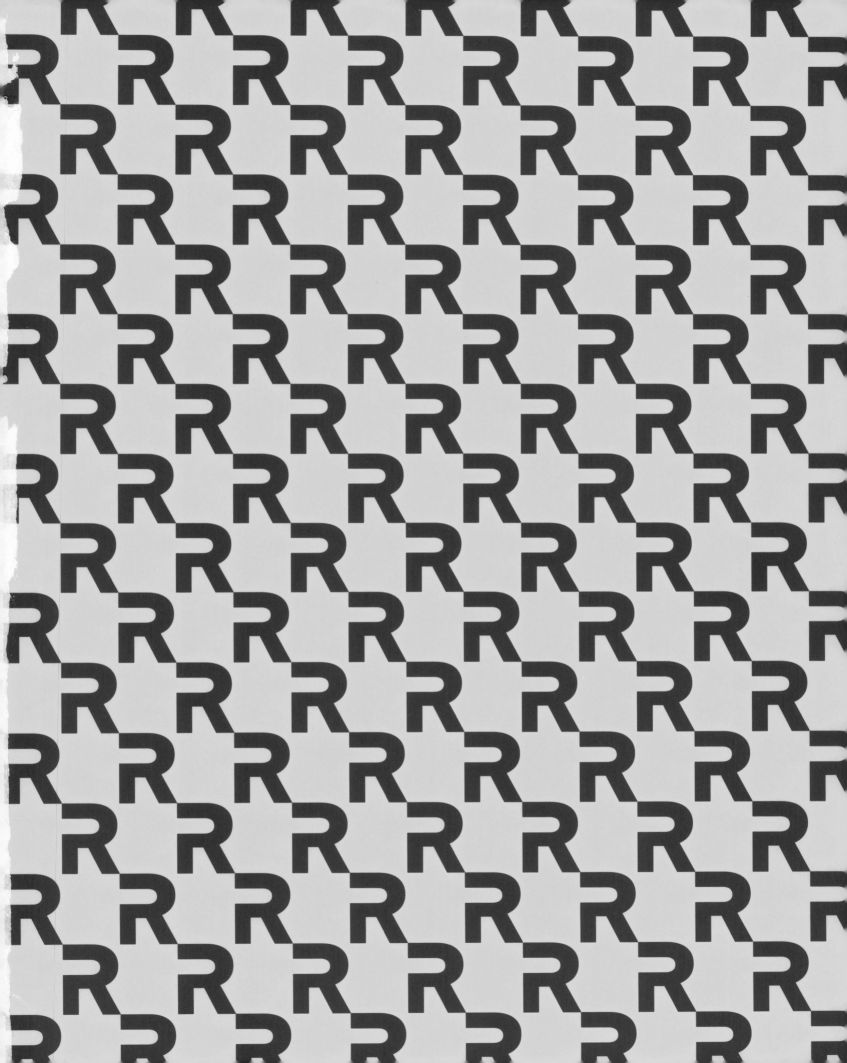

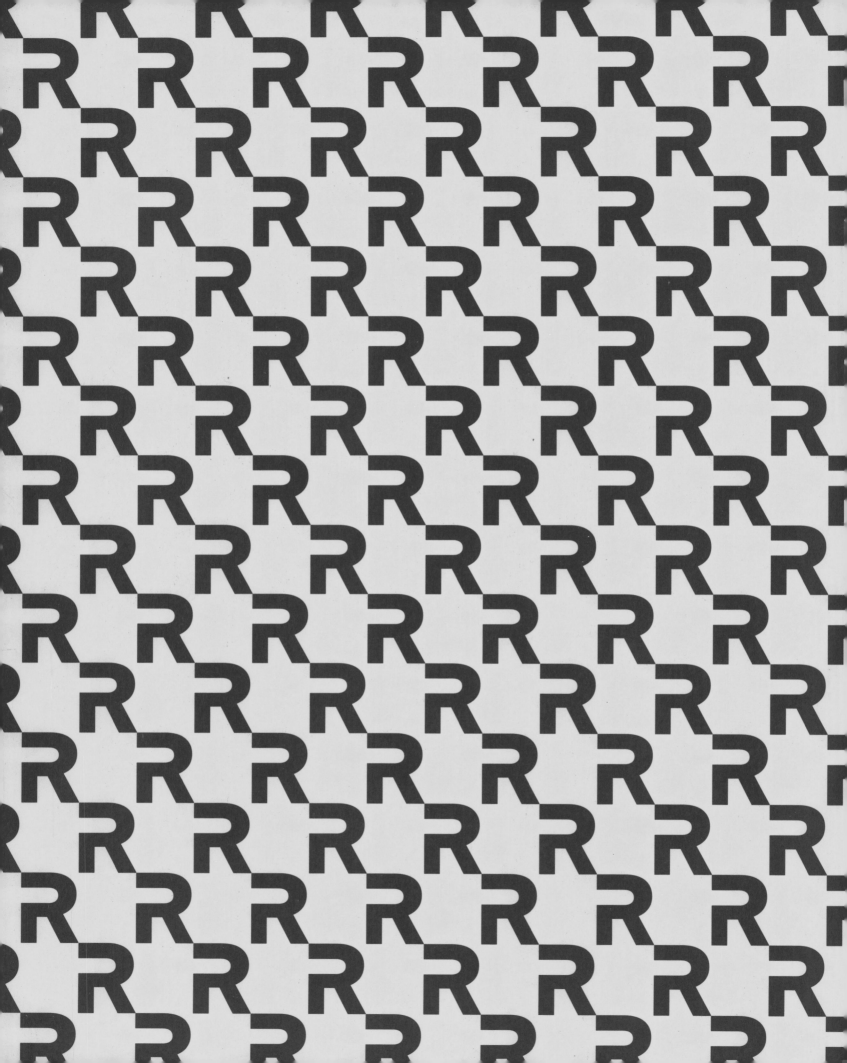